Car Mania

TUNER CARS

Ryan James

A Stingray Book

SEAHORSE PUBLISHING

Teaching Tips for Caregivers and Teachers:

This Hi-Lo book features high-interest subject matter that will appeal to all readers in intermediate and middle school grades. It may be enjoyed by students reading at or above grade level as well as by those who are looking for age-appropriate themes matched with a less challenging reading level. Hi-Lo books are ideal for ELL readers, too.

Each book appeals to a striving reader's age and maturity level. Opportunities are provided for students to read words they already know while encountering a limited number of new, high-interest vocabulary words. With these supports in place, students will read more fluently while increasing reading comprehension. Use the following suggestions to help students grow as readers.

- Encourage the student to read independently at home.
- Encourage the student to practice reading aloud.
- Encourage activities that require reading.
- Establish a regular reading time.
- Have the student write questions about what they read.

Teaching Tips for Teachers:

Before Reading

- Ask, "What do I know about this topic?"
- Ask, "What do I want to learn about this topic?"

During Reading

- Ask, "What is the author trying to teach me?"
- Ask, "How is this like something I already know?"

After Reading

- Discuss how the text features (headings, index, etc.) help with understanding the topic.
- Ask, "What interesting or fun fact did you learn?"

TABLE OF CONTENTS

WHAT IS A TUNER CAR?

A tuner car has the original factory settings of some of its parts changed to improve performance and looks.

A turbocharger may be added to an engine to give it more power.

Adding a **spoiler** can make a car look sporty and reduce **drag**.

THE FIRST TUNER CARS

People first tuned cars in the 1930s.

They made Ford Model Ts into hot rods.

A hot rod is a car that has been **modified** for increased speed and power.

FUN FACTS

Tuners are popular in the United States as well as in Italy, Japan, and Germany.

TUNER TRENDS

At the end of the 1950s, dragsters were created for racing.

These cars had huge wheels in the back and small ones in the front.

In the 1990s, people began modifying Japanese cars like the Honda Civic and Acura Integra.

They swapped out engine parts, headlamps, and exhaust pipes to make these cars faster, louder, and more stylish.

By 1999, the tuner market had reached its peak.

TUNING FOR POWER AND HEIGHT

There are different ways to tune cars.

A more powerful engine can replace the original engine. A new computer chip can change the way an engine performs.

Turbochargers can add power.

A suspension powered by **hydraulics** raises and lowers a car to make it handle better. It also lowers air resistance.

Lifting a car up and down is fun. It also attracts plenty of attention.

TUNING FOR BETTER CONTROL

A stabilizer bar is a steel spring that can connect the two wheels on an axle.

It makes the car tilt less when turning tight corners.

Short, firm lowering springs bring a car closer to the ground and make it roll and **pitch** less.

Springs like this also make the car respond quicker to the driver's steering commands.

TUNING FOR STYLE

People tune the appearance of their cars as well. Spoilers can look like wings. Paint jobs can be crazy or cool.

Changing the **rims** and tires gives a unique look. Some people make their tires lean from the top of the wheel well toward the outside of the car.

FUN FACTS

LED technology is used to create special lighting effects.

TUNER TYPES

People have created a variety of tuner cars.

A lowrider is a car with hydraulics that lift the body to make the car dance.

A rat rod looks worn-down, rusty, and unfinished.

A lead sled is a car that is very close to the ground.

MORE TUNER TYPES

DUB and donk tuner cars have oversized wheels on cars with normal ground clearance.

These vehicles are popular in hip-hop music videos.

Muscle tuner cars are two-door sedans and **coupes**.

These are created from cars that were made mainly in the 1960s and 1970s.

TUNER CARS IN ACTION

Car shows are one place where car owners can show off their tuner cars.

Enthusiasts can also be part of tuning clubs.

Some tuner cars are used for racing.

All tuner cars are one-of-a-kind vehicles.

GLOSSARY

coupes (koops): cars with two doors and a fixed roof

drag (drag): a force that slows down the forward motion of a vehicle

enthusiasts (en-THOO-zee-ists): people who are passionate about a particular subject or activity

hydraulics (hye-DRAW-liks): machines that work on power created by liquid moving through pipes under pressure

modified (MAH-duh-fyed): changed to meet a specific need

pitch (pich): to fall, plunge, or tilt

rims (rimz): the outer edges of wheels on which tires are fitted

spoiler (SPOI-lur): a device that can be attached to change the flow of air over a car

INDEX

AFTER READING QUESTIONS

1. What does it mean to tune a car?

2. What do dragsters look like?

3. Why would someone add a spoiler to their car?

4. What does a stabilizer bar do?

5. Name three reasons that people modify their cars.

ABOUT THE AUTHOR

Ryan James lives in Western North Carolina with his dog Bailey. His favorite race to watch is the Daytona 500. His dream is to own a Lamborghini. When he's not writing books, you can find him backpacking through Pisgah Forest, North Carolina.

Written by: Ryan James
Design by: Kathy Walsh
Editor: Kim Thompson

Library of Congress PCN Data
Tuner Cars / Ryan James
Car Mania
ISBN 978-1-63897-474-1 (hard cover)
ISBN 978-1-63897-589-2 (paperback)
ISBN 978-1-63897-704-9 (EPUB)
ISBN 978-1-63897-819-0 (eBook)
Library of Congress Control Number: 22022933096

Printed in the United States of America.

Seahorse Publishing Company
www.seahorsepub.com

Published in the United States
Seahorse Publishing
PO Box 771325
Coral Springs, FL 33077

SEAHORSE PUBLISHING